THERE IS
A HEALING IN
FORGIVING

Rev J Martin

DEDICATION

I dedicate this book to my family, for their constant
love and support.

CONTENTS

ACKNOWLEDGMENTS

This book would not have been possible without the support and encouragement of my family, and the inspiration from my Heavenly Father.

A special thanks to my editor and all the people a Pixal Design Studios for the lovely design work, and Amazon for providing the digital tools by which I can get my message out into the world.

Finally, I would like to thank YOU, for buying my book, may it enlighten your life and bring you peace.

Introduction

In life, we deal with people daily, in our family life, personal life, and business life. When dealing with people, there will be opportunities to get hurt. Now, we can choose to hold onto the hurt, to become bitter or angry, letting their actions affect our lives, or we can choose to forgive them and let God make it up to us.

Some of you today might have gone through some painful experiences; you feel rejected, alone, or in despair. Maybe, as you were growing up, you didn't receive the love you deserved, or maybe people were always talking down to you or making fun of you, meaning, now you have to live with the insecurities and trauma they left behind.

You may think, 'How can I forgive them for what they did to me? My friend betrayed me; I simply cannot let it go. My partner took everything from me; how can I forgive them?'

It is vital to understand; you do not forgive for their benefit. It is for your benefit.

When you forgive, you are taking away their power over you. Often, the person that hurt us is long gone, but holding onto the unforgiveness means they still have a hold on us. Don't give them that power.

If you don't forgive, if you carry around the anger or resentment, it's not hurting them; it's only hurting you. The mistake we make so often, rather than forgiving and letting down the heavy burden of unforgiveness, we hold onto it.

The only thing you are achieving by holding on to these feelings is allowing them to continue to poison your life.

The people could be out enjoying themselves; we are not hurting them by staying angry. We are only damaging our own lives, affecting our relationship with God. It's bad enough they hurt you once; don't let them continue to hurt you by staying angry.

Starting Point

If somebody cuts in front of you on the way to work, what started as a lovely morning soon turns to a horrible one. You slam the horn, your heart thumps in your chest, and you release words you wouldn't normally say.

You get into the office, still fuming, telling people what happened. They sympathize, and you calm down a little. Then, as you start your day, you are short with a customer who takes it personally and asks for the manager; before you know it, the morning has gotten worse. The day seems to spiral out of control, and you can't wait to get home.

What difference would it make if, just after it happened, you forgave the person, saying: I forgive you for pulling out in front of me; you mustn't be in your right mind. Instead of letting these angry feelings ruin my day, I will say a prayer for you. You deserve my prayers, not my anger.

This is the base level of forgiveness. If you find this hard to do, how can you be expected to forgive someone that has caused you deep emotional trauma or pain?

When we don't forgive in life, it affects us similarly to this example, but we carry the anger, not into the rest of the day, but the rest of our lives.

Mark 11:25
And when you stand praying, if you hold anything against anyone, forgive them, so that your Father in heaven may forgive you your sins."

As it says in scripture, it is in our own best interest to forgive. Jesus was telling us we are the ones God is trying to protect. We are the people who receive the most benefit from forgiveness, not the other person. A spirit of un-forgiveness compromises our daily walk with God. Forgiving others releases us from the negative feelings and allows us to receive the healing we need.

The reason we have been given specific direction is that Our Heavenly Father wants nothing blocking His love. Forgiving others spares us from the consequences of living out of an unforgiving heart.

Hebrews 10:30
For we know him who said, "It is mine to avenge; I will repay," and again, "The Lord will judge his people."

You will find that, if you turn your troubles over to God, keep a good attitude, and walk in love, He has promised to repay and judge the people that have hurt you. He has promised to make your wrongs right.

A Forgiving Mother

Scarlett Lewis' son, Jesse, was killed in the Sandy Hook Elementary School shooting in 2012. It was the biggest shooting in U.S. history. At first, she said, "It felt like her anger sapped all her strength and energy." She was angry with the shooter and with his parents for unwittingly arming him. But she chose to forgive.

She was quoted saying, "Forgiveness felt like I was given a big pair of scissors to cut the tie and regain my personal power." When we don't forgive we are emotionally attached to the person that hurt us. Forgiveness, as she said, "is being set free."

She went on to say that what started as a choice turned out to be an ongoing process. Just because you forgive does not mean a thought or memory will not set off the feelings of anger again, but as Jesse's mum said, it takes practice.

Scarlett Lewis could easily have let her son's death define her destiny; she could have attached to feelings of deep anger and resentment for the rest of her days. Instead, she became a woman of deep understanding, compassion, and love.

I share this story because it is an inspiration for me when I have been hurt. It puts my problems in perspective; I forgive, and I move on. Forgiveness is about releasing the past, so it doesn't affect the present.

Some of you have a valid reason to be angry; maybe you were mistreated when you were younger. It was out of your control, and what those people did was not right. Forgiveness doesn't mean you excuse their behavior or agree with what they did. Forgiveness means you simply let it go, so it doesn't keep replaying in your memory; it means you stop giving the pain emotional energy.

Ephesians 4:31-32
Get rid of all bitterness, rage, anger, harsh words, and slander, as well as all types of evil behavior. Instead, be kind to each other, tenderhearted, forgiving one another, just as God through Christ has forgiven you.

Every time you let a hurt consume your thoughts, going back to it, feeling how bad it was, thinking about how badly you were treated, it's like opening up an old wound; it stops the healing.

It's similar to when you were younger and cut yourself. When you took the plaster off, there was a scab; you were told picking at it would stop the healing, but it was so tempting. A wound that should have taken a week to heal took a month.

When we have been hurt, it is no different; if we don't forgive, the emotional wound takes longer to heal, and every time we let it replay in our minds or dwell on it, it opens up raw feelings.

When we approach situations this way, holding onto the pain, unwilling to let it go, something that happened 20 years ago is still as fresh in our mind. If we are not careful, it can even affect future relationships, as we always have our guard up, almost waiting to be hurt again.

I have a friend who was bullied at school when he was younger; he still holds bitterness towards the person that did it. Yes, what that bully did was wrong, but by holding on to the negative emotional energy and not forgiving, it is continuing to affect my friend's life. As much as I advise him to release it, he refuses to listen. The bitterness has taken control. My friend is still picking at his wound after 30 years.

One of You Will Betray Me

When I was at college, a close friend bullied me. On reflection, he was only my friend because I went along with everything he said. The moment I stood up for myself, saying, no sorry I can't make this Saturday was the moment he turned on me. He called me Judas for letting him down, even though I always let him know in advance.

My way of dealing with it was to avoid him, but this seemed to fuel the problem. As he was a close friend, I kept telling myself it would stop. Russell, although small, made up for it with strength and aggression. I knew speaking up for myself in front of others would come across as confrontational, so when alone, I asked him to stop. He said he would never stop. I had let him down.

I started to get a sore throat, followed by sleepless nights, which built up to anxiety. Then, one day, I made the link between what was happening at college and my ill health, explaining it all to the doctor who admitted that stress could cause numerous ailments, especially sore throats and anxiety. He advised me that if things were to change for good— I had to stand up for myself. If I didn't want a fight, then I would have to get teachers involved.

It was one of the hardest things I ever had to do, admitting to myself that I had been bullied. I never wanted to report anyone, never mind a friend; my doctor asked me to stop calling him a friend, saying, "A friend wouldn't treat you this way."

My doctor was right. I wasn't his friend; the friendship had a set of conditions I had broken— by just saying no. When I reported him, they made no scene; they simply moved me to a different class. In time, I made new friends and just kept out of his way for the remainder of the year.

It continued to hurt me for several months; I even questioned if I was to blame. This led to feelings of guilt and regret. I felt so angry inside. I didn't think I could ever forgive him for what he put me through, mentally.

Then, one day, someone gave me the following prayer; it simply transformed my life. It helped to heal the raw open wounds of losing a friendship that meant a lot to me.

Forgiveness Prayer
I forgive you, for not being,
The way I want you to be
I forgive you, and set you free.

Meaning, forgive yourself for feeling anger, bitter or guilt, and set yourself free to connect with God. It has given me great relief in times of deep hurt and confusion that I can let go of all the negative emotional baggage and embrace the essence of who I am, LOVE. This prayer has helped me throughout my life, whenever I had to deal with difficult people, people that made me feel emotions I did not enjoy.

It's important to remember that forgiveness is a process; it's not as simple as saying prayers, and it will go away. It is a process you must continuously work at.

First, you need to have the desire to forgive. Then, you will need to ask God to help you because forgiveness is difficult; part of you will fight it occasionally. Others may even tell you that you are wrong to forgive; they will put doubt in your mind.

But if you can keep with it, the negative feelings will get less and less until, one day, a memory that once spiraled you into deep anger or pain will no longer affect you.

Healing the Guilt

Some of you might feel guilty for something that wasn't your fault. You may have been mistreated when you were growing up, meaning you have a feeling that something is wrong with you, that you were to blame.

You cannot help how people treated you when you were younger. If someone took advantage of you and did you wrong, don't feel ashamed, don't feel guilty; it's not your fault— it's the other person's fault.

Hold your head up high. In the eyes of God, you did nothing wrong. You still have seeds of greatness on the inside. You still have a destiny to fulfill. Life is not always fair, but God is fair. When you learn to let go of the pain and move forward, He will repay that growth in character.

If you are in a situation where someone is doing you wrong or has done you wrong, don't get depressed;

don't give up on life. Forgive them and let it go, knowing good things are on the way.

Forgiveness exercise at the end of the book.

Dead Duck

One summer, a little boy and his sister went to visit his grandparents for two weeks. They each received a present for their schoolwork throughout the year. The little boy got a slingshot; he was over the moon with it and went straight to the wood behind the house. His grandpa had set up some targets for Johnny, but as much as he tried, he couldn't hit one; his aim was terrible.

When he got called in for supper, on his way back to the house, he spotted Grandma's pet duck sitting on the fence on the other side of the yard, a perfect silhouette against the setting sun.

It was over twice the distance he was practicing, but on impulse, he took aim and fired; the duck fell. Johnny ran over, hoping the duck had merely lost its footing. The duck was dead.

Johnny panicked, hiding the duck underneath a pile of rotten wood. When he looked up, he saw his sister; Jessica had seen it all but said nothing at the meal.

After supper, Grandma asked Jessica to help her with the dishes, to which she replied; "Johnny said he would do it tonight," whispering in Johnny's ear, "Remember the duck." So, Johnny agreed.

The next morning, Grandpa asked if the children wanted to go fishing, as it was a beautiful bright sunny day. Grandma said, "I'm sorry, but I need Jessica to help me prepare lunch." Jessica smilingly said, "Johnny was just saying how he doesn't like the water. He will stay and help you, Grandma."

Again, Jessica whispered to Johnny, "Remember the duck. "So, Johnny stayed behind to help grandma prepare the lunch while Jessica spent the whole morning relaxing in the boat.

After a full week of this, Johnny could take no more. He went to his grandma and confessed that he had killed the duck and he was sorry. "I know," she replied, hugging him. "I was standing at the kitchen window when it happened; I saw the whole thing. I have already forgiven you. I was just wondering how long you would let your sister treat you like her pet slave."

We can so easily become a slave to guilt; it can rob us of our happiness. We can say and do things we don't want to. Guilt can come in many forms; we can feel guilty for things we have done or things we think that we ought to have done.

No matter what form it takes, forgiveness is the remedy. If you caused pain or suffering by your actions, then say sorry to the person you hurt, or maybe you were not there for someone in their time of need. Until you forgive yourself and pass it over to God, it will continue to torment you.

Whatever is in your past, whatever you did or didn't do, remember it was God standing at the window. He saw the whole thing. He wants you to know that He loves you and that you are forgiven. He's just wondering how long you will let the negative forces of guilt, fear, anger, or bitterness make a slave of you. The great thing about God is, when you ask for forgiveness, you are forgiven.

Paid in Full

Matthew 6:9-13

"This, then, is how you should pray:
'Our Father in heaven, hallowed be your name,
your kingdom come, your will be done,
on earth as it is in heaven.
Give us today our daily bread.
And forgive us our debts,
as we also have forgiven our debtors.
And lead us not into temptation,
but deliver us from the evil one.

As it says in Matthew 6:12, forgive us our debts, as we also have forgiven our debtors. When Jesus mentions debts here, He is not talking about financial debts; He is talking about the times that people hurt or mistreated us.

When people do us wrong, Jesus refers to that as a debt. We feel like they owe us something. Human nature will say, you have been wronged. You need justice. You hurt me; you owe me something.

People are trying to collect a debt from another that only God can pay, and the only way God can pay that debt is for us to forgive the injustice and pass it over to Him.

That friend cannot pay you back for the months of pain and anxiety their actions caused. Your husband cannot pay you back for the years of heartache and suffering the divorce caused you and your children. Your parents cannot pay you back for all the times they were not there for you.

Only God can truly pay you back. If you want to see change and growth in your life, you need to hand over the heavy burden of unforgiveness, hand over the guilt, and hand over the anger or regret.

If you don't hand it over, thinking you must carry it on your own, you will live a very miserable and frustrating life, full of bitterness, anger, and regret. People can never give you back what they took from you; only God can repay you.

Mc. Clory and Smith

An old lady lived on a farm with her husband. It wasn't the best of land, so making a living of it was very stressful for Dan. It was tough going but manageable. Edith, his wife, loved to buy a few items each month to brighten up their home; she bought these items on credit at Mc Clory and Smith, a dry goods store in a nearby coastal town.

Dan always worried about unpaid debts, so he approached Michael Mc Clory and asked him to stop giving his wife credit. When Edith heard about this, she hit the roof and was still hitting the roof 50 years later. If she told the story once, she told it a thousand times; she would tell the story to everyone she met, even strangers that had just moved to the town.

One day her nephew asked her, "Do you not think still complaining about what happened over 50 years ago is not worse than what Uncle Dan did?" She went into a rage. Edith had paid dearly for her grudges and the bitter memories she had nourished over the years. She had paid for them with her peace of mind.

Like Edith, sometimes, rather than waiting for God to repay our debts, we pay for them with our peace of mind, going over and over what the person did. Dan had a good reason for stopping the credit, but his wife did not see it that way; she could not forgive him for the embarrassment she felt.

Benjamin Franklin, one of the founding fathers of the United States, made a mistake when he was seven years old that he remembered when he was seventy. When on holiday, his friends filled his pockets with coppers; excited with his newfound wealth, Benjamin went straight to the toyshop and bought a whistle; in his haste, he gave all his money.

Benjamin was pleased with his purchase until his siblings and cousins made him aware that he had paid nearly four times the price of the whistle. Over sixty years later, he still remembered the mistake. Even with all his success and wealth, that memory stuck in his mind. Benjamin never forgave himself for the error.

To you, this might sound childish, but we all have 'whistle' stories of our own. We all make mistakes, sometimes-simple ones, but if we don't forgive ourselves, if we keep picking at it, it never has time to heal.

Luke 17:3-4
"If your brother or sister sins against you, rebuke them; and if they repent, forgive them. Even if they sin against you seven times in a day and seven times come back to you saying, 'I repent,' you must forgive them."

Cleansing Your Spirit

As long as you are holding onto un-forgiveness, not only is it affecting your spirit, but it is keeping God from working in your life. If you are still mad at someone that's on the other side of the world, or has moved on to another loving relationship, what sense does that make?

What is the point of being mad at someone that is not even in your life anymore? Yeah, Reverend, but you do not understand what this person did. It might sound harsh, but it does not matter what they did to you; holding the feelings of anger or even hatred is not hurting them. It's only poisoning your own life. It is only prolonging your pain and misery.

Don't keep giving them your power by holding the anger and un-forgiveness in your heart. Learn to let it go; pass it over to God and let Him deal with the injustice.

Only God can truly bring justice in our lives. We may get temporary pleasure from spreading slander about a person that hurt us or getting even with them with tit-for-tat remarks, but all we are doing is blocking God from doing what He wants to do. Heal the wound.

Throughout scripture, it talks about how we are to love our enemy, and I know how hard that can be when someone purposely hurts you. It's so important to remember that it's only when we forgive, it's only when we let go of the hurt can God's healing power begin to work.

Always keep it in your mind that, when you forgive, you do not forgive for the other person's benefit; it is for your own good. You are simply doing it so God can pay you back for the wrongs done against you.

Some of you today could be trapped in the past; you are holding on to all the hurts and pains. There could be bitterness, un-forgiveness, or anger in your heart. Then you may wonder why God is not answering your prayers. First, you must do your part and let go of the negativity. Unless you do your part, then God cannot do his part.

In the Lord's Prayer it says, 'and forgive us our debts, as we also have forgiven our debtors.'

As it says in *Matthew 6:7-8*, do not repeat the same prayer over and over if you do not heed the words that are spoken. How can we rightfully expect to receive all that we ask for when we don't hold up our end of the bargain?

Life is about exchange; when you give, you will receive. When you give forgiveness, you will receive love, happiness, and peace of mind.

When you let the poison of un-forgiveness stay on the inside, you are limiting what God can do for you. You may have a good reason to feel the way you do; you may have gone through things that no person must go through.

But, to receive the true power of God, you need to do your part and forgive the hurts of the past. Stop thinking that you must sort things out on your own; realize only God can bring back the peace of mind you lost.

There is nothing the enemy would want more than for you to let one disappointment, one hurt, one betrayal ruin the rest of your life. You need to put your foot down today and say no. My destiny is too great; my future is too bright to let one injustice hold me back.

Instead, I will shake off the injustice and forgive, so I can walk into the bright future that the good Lord has in store for me.

New Beginnings

Kyle's dad was an angry and controlling man; growing up, Kyle would do whatever it took to please him and keep peace within the family. Then Kyle went to university, and without his presence, his family fell apart.

A very messy divorce followed, which led to the family property having to be divided. His dad did not stop there; he harassed the family to the point they had to sell the family home and move.

Kyle grew up thinking it was his fault. If only he had not gone to university, all might have been ok. On the inside, Kyle admitted he was bitter, he was angry, and he had never truly forgiven his father for what he put the family through.

For 15 years, he had a very destructive relationship with his dad. The more he thought about it, the more he would become bitter and angry. It got to where he had to cut him out of his life.

Kyle always felt there was something just not right; his health wasn't good, he was becoming angry, and he always needed to be in control, reminding him of his dad. Then, one day, he heard about there being a healing in forgiving, how forgiveness could release a person to move forward to feelings of love and happiness.

At 38 years of age, he visited his dad. When they met, his father's eyes lit up, then Kyle said to him, "What you did to my family and me was wrong, but I can no longer hold this poison in my heart. I have resented you for the last 15years, but I cannot live with these feelings anymore. I came here today to forgive you for your actions."

Kyle told me, when he left that day, he felt like a heavy weight had been taken off his shoulders. He felt such a lightness. For the last few years, everything seemed like a burden. Staying focused and being organized seemed close to impossible.

He explained that it felt like a new lease of life. Abundance seemed to flow into his world, not the abundance of material wealth but spiritual abundance, a joy and happiness he had thought were only destined for the young.

This happens when you keep your end of the bargain. When you forgive, it allows God's healing energy to flow into your life, making things that were once faded and old, seem brand-new.

Forgive so you can be free.

Don't let the person that hurt you keep you in the prison of unforgiveness. If you can let go of the hurt, the pain, the resentfulness, God will do for you what He did for Kyle.

He will take negative feelings and transform them into feelings of inner joy and happiness. It may have been painful, but don't waste the pain. Release it. Let God transform your life into one you are proud of living.

Maybe, like this man, someone mistreated you and your family; someone may have broken your trust or left you with three children to raise on your own. If you allow it— events like these can poison the rest of your life.

Anger and bitterness can swell within you; you may spend your days thinking of ways you can pay them back. Today, I'm advising you to forgive them, and LET IT GO. Be encouraged. God is a just God. No one else might have seen what they did to you, mentally and emotionally, but He saw it. And He will settle your disputes for you.

First, you must have the faith to hand over the hurt, the pain, and the negative feelings; forgive, so your heart is pure. When you have kept up your end of the bargain, watch what God will do for you.

He will make your wrongs right. He will turn that pain into joy. He will change the feelings of anger or bitterness to feelings of love.

Isaiah 61:7
Instead of your shame you will receive a double portion, and instead of disgrace you will rejoice in your inheritance. And so you will inherit a double portion in your land, and everlasting joy will be yours.

Rekindled Love

A young woman had a terrible relationship with her mum. As her mother had a very controlling nature, Jenna was restricted to what she could watch on TV, what she could wear, and what friends she could associate with.

She found it hard to forgive her mum for the restrictive environment she had grown up in. Jenna blamed her for the way she turned out. She found it hard to fit in socially, was quiet and insecure.

Jenna had an amazing personality but found it hard to connect with others, as the restrictive environment had affected her mental health. Finding it difficult to make friends rippled through the rest of her life.

At 18, she went to a university in another state and never returned. Her unforgiveness over the years turned to resentment. On reading one of my books, she contacted me with her story. She realized it was time to forgive, as holding onto the negative feelings was affecting her health and her relationship with her own little girl. But now, at 26, it had been eight years, and she didn't know how to approach her mother.

I advised her, if she found it hard to meet face to face, she should send a letter and see if she got a response, letting her mother know the reasons she found it hard to return.

Jenna got a heartfelt reply from her mum. Her mother opened up to her, confessing her sister and friends had mentally abused her when she was young; she too found it hard to connect with people.

She apologized for how she treated Jenna, admitting she let her bitterness and anger ruin their relationship; she hoped that, one day, Jenna could find it in her heart to forgive her.

Jenna's mother said, the last six years not knowing where her daughter was, was the hardest of her life. It made her return to church; she rediscovered the bible, asked for forgiveness for not being the mother that her child deserved, and prayed the moment would come that they would be reunited.

Jenna was deeply moved by the letter and met her mum the following Saturday. She said the moment they met was one of the most memorable moments of her life. The feeling of love from her mother was better than she ever imagined.

People that hurt you often have been hurt; Jenna's mum had a lot of anger and bitterness she never released. She had never forgiven those that hurt her.

Instead, she held onto it and passed it down to her daughter.

Moral High Ground

What really shows strength of character is when we realize the people that hurt us have deep unresolved issues of their own. If someone lashed out at you, abandoned you, or mistreated you, often they had similar things done to them.

Now, this does not excuse what they did, but it's important to remember they only did it because someone on their journey hurt them. Somebody didn't give them what they needed.

If you take this merciful approach, saying, "I know what they did to me was wrong. I know it wasn't right, but I am not going to try to repay the wrongdoing. I am not going to try to get revenge. God, I'm asking you to heal them, give them what they need."

When you can bless those that hurt you, seeing from their perspective, you will see God show up in amazing ways to pay you back for that compassion.

John 20:23

If you forgive the sins of any, they are forgiven them; if you retain the sins of any, they are retained.

When we retain something, it means we hold on to it. What I think Jesus meant by this passage was, when we hold onto the wrongs that people have done against us, when we retain their sin in un-forgiveness, when we

27

nurture it, it can grow, meaning we do that same wrong to others.

If we have been made to feel guilty for most of our lives, we can easily teach that guilt to our children, as it's the only way we know.

When you don't forgive, it's easy to become that which you hate. If you make others feel guilty for not spending time with you, the little time they spend will seem too much for them, as they are constantly reminded of their shortcomings.

This is why it is so important to forgive and let go. The wrongs we hold onto, the sins we retain, can produce in us exactly what we don't want. If you have been brought up in an environment of anger, fear, doubt or worry, don't let that negativity get on the inside of you.

I have heard men in their seventies saying they wish they could go back and kill certain people that hurt them in their teens. These same men have problems with their health, carrying that anger, bitterness, and resentment for over 50 years. Is it any wonder? What a waste of a beautiful life.

It can be difficult to forgive; it takes great mental strength and courage; it shows a great depth of character, a great maturity. I would like you to know you have seeds of greatness within you, but you have to stand up and be counted.

Release the true power of God into your life today by forgiving all those that hurt you.

Seventy Seven Times

If people take advantage of you or hurt you— cross them off your list but don't try to get even. When you try to get even, more often than not, you will come off worse than the person that mistreated you.

You may ask, how can trying to get even hurt me?

Well, many people's way to get even is to shut a person out of their life. They blank them in the street; they tell their friends and family to have nothing to do with them.

Holding these feelings within leads to resentment, the number one cause of hypertension (high blood pressure), which can cause many other illnesses.

When Jesus said, "Love your enemies," He was not only preaching moral principles; He was preaching 20th-century medicine. When he said, "Forgive your brother not seven times but seventy-seven times," he was telling you and me how to avoid stress, anxiety, high blood pressure, stomach ulcers, and many other ailments.

Jesus's words can even help people with their looks; I know people so infected with anger and bitterness that it shows in their faces; there is a pale, blank look absent of spirit.

Nothing would improve their looks more than a heart full of forgiveness, tenderness, and love. Resentment or deep anger can even affect the enjoyment of food; the bible sums it up in Proverbs 15:17, Better a small serving of vegetables with love than a fattened calf with hatred.

The people that hurt us would love to see the effect of their actions, how it was changing our spirit, making us tired, angry, or depressed. We need to love ourselves enough not to permit our enemies to control our happiness, our health, and our looks.

I hope you are getting a sense of why Jesus spoke so much about forgiveness; it is probably one of the purest forms of healing in modern medicine.

Financial Sense

An older gentleman with a very successful business came asking for some advice, as one of his main clients hurt him in his personal life. As the famous saying goes, 'don't mix business with pleasure.'

He knew it did not make good business sense, but he was about to cancel him as a client; he had come to me as his wife had advised him to get a spiritual opinion on a matter that could cost his business up on $100,000 a year.

He showed me the letter he would send. It made the hairs on my neck stand up. The page felt heavy with anger. I walked to the window to open it, as I needed fresh air to calm down. "Well, from your reaction, I take it I shouldn't send that letter."

When I finally settled down, I recited Matthew 18:21-22 and advised him to rewrite the letter, thanking his client for the last 10 years of business, explaining to him the power of forgiveness even in business. During the conversation that followed, he saw things from my perspective, how losing one major deal could affect his company.

Matthew 18:21-22
Then Peter came to Jesus and asked, "Lord, how many times shall I forgive my brother or sister who sins against me? Up to seven times?" Jesus answered, "I tell you, not seven times, but seventy-seven times

Three weeks later, he returned, thanking me for the advice, saying, "You will not believe what your advice has done." He told me that his client returned the letter, telling him he would double his order for the next month due to a bad supplier.

Forgiveness applies to all areas of life; it can soften people's hearts to love, which can open up more meaningful relationships and opportunities.

Take Back the Power

I had a young man tell me recently how he had to break off a relationship with a girl due to her jealous nature. She would hassle him from the moment he came home from work to the moment he would go to bed. Who had he seen and talked to throughout the day.

He admitted he had a temper, which seemed to escalate under these conditions. Rather than strike her, he smashed phones against walls and put his fist through doors.

To make matters worse, she threatened to tell her brother, who might injure him, what he had done if he ever dared to leave her. This young man was caught in a cycle of mental torture from which he could not escape. He loved her deeply but was pushed to the point he couldn't handle it any longer, finally getting the strength to walk away.

This put her over the edge; she couldn't live with him or without him. Rather than letting things settle, she threatened him again, harassing him daily, spreading slander and lies.

Rick came in a bad mental state, not knowing what to do. I advised him not to believe the lies she was spreading, not to be sucked into her web of fear and negativity but to believe what God said about him.

Psalms 3:5-6
Trust in the LORD with all your heart and lean not on your own understanding; in all your ways submit to him, and he will make your paths straight.

Negative people and those of little faith want to pull us down at every opportunity. They want us to get angry, upset, depressed, and live in fear. They want us to hold unforgiveness and bitterness in our hearts, for it to poison our lives. They are not happy, and they don't want you to be happy.

He was living in deep fear; he painted her brother to be as big as Goliath. I told him of the story of David, how an entire army of trained men feared one man. Then David, who had a profound faith in God, went out to face Goliath with little more than a slingshot, and with God's help, David took down Goliath.

David was not unique, but he had something the ten thousand soldiers hadn't; David had faith that God was on his side, and all would be ok.

1 Corinthians 6:19

Do you not know that you are God's temple and that God's Spirit lives in you?

When someone makes us feel intimidated, fear can quickly grow to anger. Anger is a red mist; in the heat of the moment, we can say and do things that only escalate the problem.

I advised Rick to walk away from the situation and cut all contact; I explained it would not be easy but the only thing to do; if people try to take advantage of you or hurt you, cross them off your list but don't try to get even.

Living with Regret

If we keep putting off forgiveness, a loved one can pass away, meaning the opportunity to forgive is gone. The weight of forgiveness weighs ounces, but the weight of regret weighs tonnes.

I can sum up regret; I wish I had spent more time with a loved one. I wish I had said sorry sooner. I wish I told my friend how much I loved them. When we have the chance of sorting things out with a loved one or friend, be the bigger person and say sorry; forgive them for their actions.

An accident can take a person away from us today; I would rather scare you than you live for the next 40-50 years wishing you exchanged a few words.

My mom's aunt, who is now 86years old, lived her life in the service of others and did brilliant work. She would go to the far end of the world if she thought it would help anyone, and she did.

But now, to be in her company is a very sad experience. She says on many occasion, "I feel very down and depressed thinking of the past, all the things I wish I could change, the things I would have done differently."

She had a row with her sister over the family estate when her parents died. They both said some harsh words; her sister moved away, and they never spoke again. Her sister died without them ever making peace.

Now, she speaks about it often, saying, "I wanted to forgive her, but I kept putting it off. Why did I do that?" It is visible on her face that the regret is constantly on her mind.

A few simple words like, "Sorry, please forgive me," would have changed everything. She would now have no regret and live out the remainder of her life with peace of mind.

Why do we make life so difficult? Why can we not heed the words of Jesus, "I tell you, not seven times, but seventy-seven times?"

Sometimes, we have decisions to make, but we keep putting them off. By taking action, we know things would change for the better; we would be happier and regain our peace of mind; why then do we not do it?

My great aunt is a woman of great faith, attends church every week. Her faith is the cornerstone of her life, but why did she not apply what Jesus said?

Most people don't forgive because they think they have done nothing wrong, or they think the other person should be the one to forgive. Both people hold onto the unforgiveness, letting it poison their lives.

If, like in this woman's case, the person that hurt you is gone, you need to forgive yourself for holding the feelings within you; release them and pass them over to God. If you still have the opportunity to offer forgiveness, make that call today. Be under no illusion it will be easy, but the rewards— I cannot sum up in words. The regaining of a loving bond cannot be measured. Release the negative feelings of anger or bitterness.

Taking this step takes great character and integrity. Forgiving others does not mean you are weak; in the eyes of God, you are strong and of mighty courage; you have listened to His words. Always remember that you are doing it for your benefit; you are keeping up your end of the bargain.

Sorry has only five letters, but it is one of the hardest words to say; a healing energy is within it that can heal even the deepest wound. Words of forgiveness have healing power, for the one that says them and the one that receives them; they heal everyone; they generate growth within.

Jesus said in Matthew 5:39, 'If anyone slaps you on the right cheek, turn to them the other cheek also.' Jesus was referring to forgiveness; if someone hurts you, forgive them; do not hold the negative feelings in your heart. Turning the other cheek means you have forgiven them, giving them another chance. If they hurt you again, distance yourself and move towards those that motivate and encourage you.

You will find, as you walk on a more spiritual path, those that walk beside you will be less in numbers. This does not mean you are on the wrong track. A life without anger, fear, and aggression seems impossible to most people because they have allowed themselves to be consumed by negativity. Heeding the word of God and forgiving those that hurt us allows a healing energy to flow into our lives.

The Power of Dreams

In scripture, Joseph's brothers sold him into slavery out of jealousy of his dreams. Their actions ruined his life. Joseph could have easily felt angry, resentful, and he would have been justified in feeling bitter, but he knew God would make it up to him. Joseph knew great things were in his destiny, and for them to be fulfilled, there could be no negativity in his heart.

As one thing after another kept happening to him, he was finally thrown into prison for 13 years for a crime he didn't even commit.

When he was in prison, Joseph overheard two men talking, a baker and a cupbearer; they both had vivid dreams and were trying to work out what they meant. When he told the cupbearer that his dream meant he would be released in three days and be a cupbearer to the pharaoh, the cupbearer jumped around saying, "That is wonderful news; how can I ever repay you?" To which Joseph suggested, "Perhaps, one day, you could ask the pharaoh to pardon me."

The cupbearer agreed saying, "If what you say is true and I get my freedom, I'll be sure to put a good word in for you." The cupbearer got out in a few days as Joseph predicted, but he forgot all about him.

How often have you helped someone, giving your time and energy, for it to be forgotten? Then when they get back on their feet, and you need help, these same people forget how you helped them.

Well, that's how Joseph probably felt, and he could have felt angry and bitter, but he took the moral high ground, knowing good was coming. He knew God would bring balance to his life by not allowing negative feelings to cloud his mind.

Two years later, the pharaoh had two dreams that not even the wisest men in Egypt could interpret; the cupbearer, remembering Joseph, told the pharaoh of a man he met in prison with the gift of reading dreams.

Joseph was called before the pharaoh, and with God's help, he interpreted the pharaoh's dreams, telling him there were seven years of great abundance to be followed by seven years of famine. Pleased with the news, the pharaoh gave him the position of the high governor, second in command of Egypt.

If Joseph had kept un-forgiveness in his heart, he would never have the wisdom to interpret the pharaoh's dreams; he would never have fulfilled his destiny. Like with Joseph, if you allow God to make the wrongs right, He will always bring you real justice.

As high governor, Joseph was to collect all the food for the seven years of famine. When the seven years of famine came, his brothers were sent to Egypt to get food, as it was the only place with supplies.

Joseph instantly recognized his brothers, but when he approached them, he realized they didn't recognize him dressed as a governor. When he finally revealed himself to them, they fell in fear, pleading for him to go easy on them.

Instead of paying them back for selling him into slavery, leaving him without a younger brother and father for most of his life, he forgave them and invited them to come live with him in Egypt.

Each of us has had unfair things happen to us. People may have treated you like Joseph's brothers treated him. Their actions led to you having a bad start in life, but if you hand that anger and hurt over to God and let Him deal with it, He will always bring you out ahead.

It does you no good to hate somebody that has done wrong against you; if anything, it will only damage your health and peace of mind. Learn to cast away negative feelings and move on. Don't let the poison of un-forgiveness contaminate the rest of your life.

The rewards of forgiveness are beyond your understanding.

Repaying the Debt

In the Gospel of Matthew, Jesus told his disciples a parable about a king who wanted to settle the debts of his slaves. As he began to settle them, a slave was brought before him that owed 10,000 talents.

But since he did not have the means to repay the money, his King commanded him to be sold, with his wife and children and all he had. The slave fell to the ground, saying, 'Have patience with me and I will repay you everything.'

The King felt compassion for the slave and released him and forgave him the debt. But upon his release, the slave found one of his fellow slaves who owed him a hundred denarii, and he seized him and choked him, saying, 'Pay back what you owe.'

His fellow slave fell to the ground and pled with him, saying, 'Have patience with me, and I will repay you,' but he was unwilling, and got him thrown in prison until he could pay back what was owed.

When the King found out what happened, he summoned him, and said, 'You wicked slave, I forgave you your debt because you pleaded with me. Should you not also have had mercy on your fellow slave, in the same way, that I had mercy on you?' Moved with anger, the king handed him over to the torturers until he repaid all that was owed him.

Jesus finished the parable by saying, "My heavenly Father will also do the same to you if each of you does not forgive your brother from your heart."

When we don't forgive, that un-forgiveness creates a block in our lives; we may not be handed over to torturers, but we may lose our peace of mind; over time that blockage could lead to illness or pain.

The sad realization is, people feel that someone owes them for all the pain and suffering they have been through; holding that un-forgiveness (otherwise known as resentment or bitterness) leads to illness, stiffness, and pain, but they still want to be paid what is owed to them. People waiting to be paid back live a frustrated life.

The Three Kings

I was recently talking to a man who got divorced 18 years ago; all but one of his sons was speaking to him. What about the third son? "He will only meet me one day a week. Oh, I let him know what will happen if he shuts me out like his brothers."

From listening to this man for little more than an hour, it was apparent why his three sons were having a terrible relationship with him. He talked about them as if they owed him something.

This man was bitter; he had missed out on his children growing up, but rather than treasuring the moments he had now, he was pushing them away with the bitterness and anger. He still expected them to pay him back for all the years he had lost.

I told him, when he forgives them for the past and treasures each moment he has with them in the present, God would take his life to a whole new level.

People may have done you wrong; it may have been their fault, but it is not their fault they cannot pay you back. If you spend your life trying to get from others what only God can give, it will ruin that relationship and the next and the next. Like with the slave in the parable, instead of looking for your hundred denarii the next time someone hurts you, remember God has let you off with all your debts.

So, the next time you see that person that lied to you, remember God has let you off with all your debts. When you see that friend that betrayed you, remember God has let you off with your debts.

It's very liberating to say, no one owes me anything; they may have hurt me, bullied me, or cheated me, but I know when I hand that pain over to God, my debts will be paid in full.

Changing Tides

Why don't you set a new standard for your family; rise up and make a difference. Are you going to hold onto the anger or bitterness and pass it down to the next generation, or are you going to let it go and take your life to a new level?

When filled with feelings of anger, resentment, guilt, or regret, we can easily let these feelings grow within us to affect the relationships in our lives. If your parents were mean and abusive, the enemy wants you to be mean and abusive; if your parents argued and fought all the time, he wants you to argue and fight all the time.

Someone of great character must step up and break the negative cycle. Somebody must have the courage to say, enough is enough; I don't care who hurt me or how wrong it was; from this day forth, I refuse to live in the prison of un-forgiveness.

Somewhere along the line, someone must say, I'm no longer going to live angry and mad at the world; instead, I will hand the debts over to God and let Him deal with the pain, let Him make my wrongs right.

If you find this hard, let this be your daily prayer. Dear Lord, give me the strength to do what is right.

Life is too short to hold onto the hurts and pains of the past. Health is too valuable to allow something that happened years ago to affect your peace of mind.

No matter how hard it maybe for you to forgive, you must forgive. It's too easy to sit around and have pity on yourself; it's so easy to blame everyone else for your life turning out the way it did.

When we hold onto un-forgiveness, we stop the flow of God's healing energy.

From today, change your attitude; look forward to the clarity of mind that will come when that negative memory no longer has a hold on you. Expect God to reward you for your forgiveness by turning your life around.

Jesus spoke often about the importance of forgiveness; listening to his teaching is refreshing and motivational, but it is not until you apply his teaching that you will be a witness to the kingdom of heaven, which he so fondly spoke of.

The Runaway

Amy grew up in Woolsington, Newcastle, England. In her late teenage years, she fell into a pattern of long running battles with her parents. They didn't approve of the way she dressed, and her friends weren't exactly her parent's first choice. They were furious when she stayed out all night without so much as a phone call.

One night, after a huge fight, she screamed, "I hate you both!" and ran upstairs, locking herself in her bedroom. In the early hours of the morning, when her parents had gone to sleep, Amy got dressed, packed a bag, and went down to the kitchen. Opening the kitchen drawer, she found her parent's wallets. Taking the credit cards, the cash, and their bankbook, then taking her bag, she hopped in a taxi and headed for Newcastle.

When she got there, she waited on the doorstep of the Lloyds Bank so she could be the first through the door. She forged her mother's signature and withdrew £10,000 from her parent's investment account and got a train to London.

Pretty soon, she was enjoying the high life – she had a new group of friends, plenty of booze, late nights, no parent's hassling her about what she was wearing. For the first time in her young life, she could do what she wanted.

Meanwhile, back home, her parents were frantic. Her mother had to pack shelves at night to pay off the credit card debt, and the money set aside for her sister's university fees was gone. The police were notified and the streets searched – first Newcastle, then nearby towns and cities. Her parents didn't know what happened. They feared the worst.

Amy's wild life soon led to her being addicted to cocaine, and soon, the £10,000 was gone. With the credit cards cancelled, she moved into a squat and sold herself for sex. One day, when she was walking in central London, she saw a poster headed, "Have you seen this girl?" Below the heading was a photo of her – at least how she used to look.

The poster had her parent's phone number on it, asking for anyone with information to call. Amy ripped down the poster, folded it up, and put it in her pocket.

The months passed, then the years. Amy had been careless one time too many. At first, she wrote it off as a sickness, but the illness persisted. She went to the free clinic to discover she had contracted HIV. Not even the brothel wanted anything to do with her now.

As she sat lonely, tired, and hungry in the squat, she looked at the poster she'd saved for the last few years, thinking back to her previous life— a typical schoolgirl in a middle-class suburban Newcastle family.

It triggered memories of family holidays when she was young, the carefree moments running with her father and sister on the beach, of her sister holding her in her arms listening to all her boyfriend troubles. "God, why did I leave that life?" she said to herself. All she wanted to do was return to Newcastle.

She phoned home and just got the answer phone a few times, but found it hard to leave a message. Getting the answer phone again, she said, "Mum, Dad it's Amy. I was wondering if I might come home. I'm catching the last train from London and will be in Newcastle about midnight. If you are not there, well, I will work something out."

On the train the next day, Amy questioned her plan. What if her parents didn't get the message? They were never good with technology. What if they were in shock? It had been 10 years. How were they going to react to finding out she had HIV, that their daughter was a disappointment? If they turned up, what was she going to say?

As the train pulled into Newcastle station just after midnight, Amy looked out along the platform, but it was too dark outside to see. Her heart beat faster in her chest; she never thought she would set foot in Newcastle again.

Amy stepped out of the train not knowing what to expect. She looked to her right, and there was nothing but an empty platform, but before she could turn the other way, she heard her name called in unison. She whipped her head around; there was her mum, dad, and her sister with her baby girl, along with most of her family.

Her mum and dad ran towards her with open arms. Amy froze to the spot as her parents grabbed her with such force they almost knocked her over. "Mum, Dad, I'm sorry," she said with tears rolling down her face.

"Hush child. Forget the apologies. All we care about is that you're home. I just want to hold you. Come on; everyone's waiting – we've got a big party organized." Amy found herself awash in a sea of family love she had not known for over ten years.

Based on a *fictional* story by Philip Yancey, *What's So Amazing About Grace*, paralleling the story of the prodigal son.

I have concluded with this story because it shows that forgiveness can be the turning point in a person's life. Amy's parents could easily have held onto the bitterness and resentment, having to pay back what she had taken from them, letting the feelings grow in their hearts until all the love for their daughter was gone.

But, if she had stepped off that train to an empty platform, it would have been the beginning of the end for poor Amy. Like Amy's parents in this story, we too have the power to change our lives and the lives of others with forgiveness.

Life is too short to go through it carrying emotional baggage, carrying all the pains, hurts, and regrets of the past. You can carry it, but it will cost you, and the longer you carry it, the more expensive it will get.

Your peace of mind will be the first high price you will pay, then your joy and happiness; eventually your health will fail, which will keep you from enjoying your life to the fullest. Is holding all that emotional baggage worth it?

People will always say, but they don't deserve forgiveness, but to them, I say— you are probably right, but guess what, YOU DO.

Matthew 6:14-15

For if you forgive other people when they sin against you, your heavenly Father will also forgive you. But if you do not forgive others their sins, your Father will not forgive your sins.

Divine Grace

When most people think of forgiveness, they think they have to forgive another person. They believe forgiveness must be given to someone else. It's almost like, if you betrayed me, if you hurt me, I have to be the bigger person and forgive you.

There is almost a sense of entitlement and authority. You're wrong. I'm right, so I forgive you. I would like you to remove yourself from that idea; instead, get into your heart. You do this by realizing forgiveness is not for the other person; it is for you.

Even if the person that hurts you apologizes, until you release the hurtful feelings, forgiveness does not take place. The power is always with you.

When you think of the word forgive, think of giving away, letting go. What do you need to give away? What has been holding you back from expressing your inner love, joy, and happiness?

God's love is infinite. He is with us 24/7. What blocks us from connecting with Him are the layers and layers of beliefs, fears, and hurts we hold onto. Give them away; let them go. You don't need them anymore. The moment you do this, a weight will drop off your shoulders, a massive weight.

When that person hurt you, you abandoned yourself, and you did so to deal with the situation. I don't want to judge you; you did what you needed to do, but you abandoned that part of you connected to God, the inner child.

You need to remember the inner child must be expressed, needs to heal. Even if you remove yourself from your circumstances, that inner child is still inside you, and if you don't embrace that part of you, if you don't allow him or her to express their pain, that pain will repeat certain patterns in your life.

If you get into a relationship, you may never fully trust the person you are in love with. If you follow your dreams, you may never feel your good enough. You may not have many friends because you almost expect people to hurt you. There will be intimacy issues you will have for a long time. I know, because I have gone through it myself.

One thing I recommend is to sit down when feeling at your worst, with a note pad or the digital alternative, put on some emotional music, and just let out what you feel; release all the emotions.

Express what you need to express, writing what you would like to say to a certain person or persons, hold nothing back. What comes out comes from a place of anger, pain, neglect, and abandonment.

When I used to do this, my eyes would fill up; those tears expressed the energy I had locked deep within, all the hurts I had not resolved. It is valuable to express your emotions, instead of suppressing them, as these feelings lead to anger, resentment, bitterness, and depression.

Express them and pass them over to God, saying, 'you know what I have been through; you know how much a family member, neighbor, or spouse has hurt me; you know that it wasn't right— God I'm not holding onto it anymore. I am releasing it all to you.'

Do this, and you cannot imagine the joy and happiness that will flow into your life. Like releasing a feather into the wind, you will experience a freedom you never knew was possible.

It will be hard initially due to the withdrawal process, but it will be worth it. God will make your wrongs right; He will pay you back for what the people that hurt you stole. You will come out better than you were before.

This is the work few people are prepared to do, but if they get the courage to do it, their whole life changes, not because their circumstances change, but their relationship with God. That is the power of forgiveness; it is a healing energy that can transform your life.

Forgive. Let go. Let God's energy flow.

ABOUT THE AUTHOR

I live on the northwest coast of Ireland. I use this medium to share my true voice. I wish to enlighten others and help them to see that God wants the very best for them. We often make it hard for him to enter our lives as we focus on the dark clouds rather than the silver lining.

In this growing digital frontier I just want to shed a little light out into the world to light up peoples lives in the hope that they to will help inspire others which will slowly but surely change the world, even in a small way.

My Other Books

The Power Of Letting Go
The Power Of Choice
The Power Of Words
The Power of Faith Can Move Mountains
Let Angels be your Guide
Make Space for God

Printed in Great Britain
by Amazon

17639625R00038